Made in United States
Orlando, FL
23 May 2024

47142703R00080

GENESIS
FOUNDATION BOOK OF THE BIBLE

MIKE MAZZALONGO

STUDENT WORKBOOK

BibleTalk.TV

**DOWNLOAD
OUR APP**

Genesis

Foundation Book of the Bible

Mike Mazzalongo

A 50-lesson series that covers all 50 chapters of Genesis. From creation to the flood and on to Abraham finishing with Joseph in Egypt. A complete study of the first book in the Bible.

bibletalk.tv/genesis

Table of Contents

1. Book of Origins

In this introductory lesson we will examine the 14 different things and events whose origins are found in the book of Genesis.

Series objectives:

1. _____

2. _____

3. _____

I. Genesis = Origins

1. _____

_____

_____

2. _____

_____

_____

3. _____

_____

_____

4. _____

_____

_____

5. _____

_____

_____

6. _____

_____

_____

7. _____

_____

_____

8. _____

_____

_____

9. _____

_____

_____

10. _____

_____

_____

11. _____

_____

_____

12. _____

_____

_____

13. _____

_____

_____

14. _____

_____

_____

II. Genesis and the Bible

_____

_____

_____

SCIENTIFIC FACTS OR PRINCIPLE	DATE OF DISCOVERY	BIBLICAL LOCATION
Taxonomical classifications of matter 1. Time - 2. Energy - 3. Force - 4. Space - 5. Mass	1735	Gen. 1
Oceans lie in one bed		Gen.1:9
Both man and woman possess seed of life	17th century	Gen. 3:15 & 22:18
Most seaworthy ship design is 30:5:3	1860	Gen. 6
Infinite number of stars	1940	Gen. 15:5
Certain animals carry diseases harmful to man	16th century	Lev. 11
Early diagnosis of leprosy	17th century	Lev. 13:1-9
Quarantine for disease control	17th century	Lev. 13:45-47
Blood of animals carries disease	17th century	Lev. 17:13
Blood necessary for survival of life	19th century	Lev. 17:11 / Deut. 12:23
There is a place void of stars in the north	19th century	Job 26:7
Earth is held in place by invisible forces	1650	Job 26:7
Air has weight	16th century	Job 28:25
Light is a particle (has mass, a photon)	1932	Job 38:19
Radio astronomy (stars give off signals)	1945	Job 38:7
Oceans contain freshwater springs	1920	Job 38:16
Snow has material value	1905, 1966	Job 38:22
Using electricity to carry sound		Job 38:35
Arcturus and other stars move through space	19th century	Job 38:32
Oceans have natural paths in them - Matthew Fontaine Murray	1854	Psalm 8:8
Moon gives no light		Isaiah 13:10
Water cycle	17th century	Eccl. 1:7
Dust is important for survival	1935	Isa. 40:12
The earth is round	15th century	Isa. 40:22 / Prov. 8:27
Day and night occur simultaneously on earth	15th century	Lk. 17:31-34
Earth rotates on axis		James 1:17

2. Authorship and Division of Genesis

This second lesson will examine the various theories about the authorship of Genesis and it's natural and imposed divisions.

Intro – Review two basic points:

1. _____

2. _____

_____

_____

I. Authorship

Three main authorship explanations about how Genesis was produced:

1. Group of writers_____

_____

_____

"Higher criticism" _____

_____

_____

Documentary hypothesis _____

_____

_____

2. Moses as the author - three possibilities:

- _____
- _____
- _____

3. Moses as compiler and editor _____

_____

_____

_____

II. Division of Genesis

_____

_____

_____

1. Overview Division

_____

_____

    A. God and the world – Genesis 1-11

_____

_____

_____

    B. God and His people – Genesis 12-50

_____

_____

_____

2. General Divisions

Divided by generations

_____

_____

_____

10 Generations

1. Generations of heaven and earth – 1:1-2:4 _____

_____

_____

2. Generations of Adam – 2:4b-5:1 _____

_____

_____

3. Generations of Noah – 5:1-6:9 _____

_____

_____

4. Generations of sons of Noah – 6:9-10:1 _____

_____

_____

5. Generations of Shem – 10:1-11:10 _____

_____

_____

6. Generations of Terah – 11:10-11:27 _____

_____

_____

7. Generations of Isaac – 11:27-25:11 _____

_____

_____

9. Generations of Jacob – 25:19-37:1 _____

_____

_____

10. Generations of the sons of Jacob – Genesis 37:2-Exodus 1:1 _____

_____

_____

_____

_____

3. The Foundational Verse of the Bible

In this lesson we will demonstrate how the very first verse of the Bible refutes the major philosophies that try to explain man's existence without reference to God. (Genesis 1:1)

Intro – Review of Genesis

1. Inspiration _____
2. Nature _____
3. Author _____
4. Division _____

I. Foundational Verse – Verse 1

_____

_____

Henry Morris – "Genesis Record" _____

_____

7 Philosophies Refuted by Genesis 1:1

1. Atheism _____

   _____

2. Pantheism _____

   _____

3. Polytheism _____

   _____

4. Materialism _____

   _____

5. Dualism _____

   _____

6. Humanism _____

   _____

7. Evolution _____

   _____

Other philosophies that Genesis 1:1 refutes include:

Naturalism _____

Deism _____

Agnosticism _____

Monism _____

Determinism _____

Pragmatism _____

Nihilism _____

_____

_____

_____

II. The Words in Genesis 1:1

God _____

_____

Created _____

_____

Heavens _____

_____

Earth _____

_____

In the beginning _____

_____

_____

If you were translating Genesis 1:1 into modern scientific English you could say,

"The transcendent _____ Godhead called into _____

the _____, _____, _____ universe."

4. Old Earth vs. Young Earth

In this lesson, we will discuss the major arguments supporting the young (6,000 to 10,000 years) versus the old (millions to billions of years) age of the earth.

Intro – Scientists say that the universe is comprised of _____ - _____ - _____

_____

_____

_____

Genesis 1:1 refutes _____

_____

_____

I. Age of the Earth

Old Earth _____

_____

Young Earth _____

_____

_____

1. Old View of Earth

_____

_____

_____

Geological Record:

_____

_____

_____

_____

Old Earth Theory Problems

A. Have to assume contradictory ideas:

- Something comes from _____

- Matter is _____

- Time and chance _____

B. Have to accept conflict between what is proposed and what is observed.

_____

_____

                       - Geological Record _____

                       _____

                       _____

- Absence of "links" _____

_____

2. Young View of Earth

No philosophical problems _____

_____

No observable contradictions _____

_____

Young earth model (6,000 – 10,000 years) is supported by:

1. _____

2. _____

3. _____

Summary

_____

_____

_____

5. The Gap Theory in Creationism

This lesson will begin a review of various alternative interpretations of the creation portion of the book of Genesis.

Intro – Review

Old earth _____

_____

_____

    Problems:

    A. Theoretical _____

_____

_____

    B. Geological _____

_____

_____

New Earth _____

_____

_____

    Proofs:

    A. _____

_____

_____

    B. _____

_____

_____

    C. _____

_____

_____

I. Gap Theory

Proposes a long time-gap between Genesis 1:1 and Genesis 1:2.

_____

_____

_____

Gap Theory:

1. God _____

   _____

   _____

2. Satan _____

   _____

   _____

3. God _____

   _____

   _____

The main purpose of the Gap Theory was to _____

_____

_____

Problems with Gap Theory

1. Scientific _____

_____

_____

2. Biblical _____

_____

_____

Romans 5:12 _____

_____

_____

I Corinthians 15:21 _____

_____

_____

II. Study of Genesis 1:2

"And the earth was..." _____

_____

_____

_____

"...formless and void..."

_____

_____

_____

"...darkness was on the face (surface) of the deep."

_____

_____

_____

"The Spirit of God moved over the surface of the waters..."

_____

_____

_____

"RACHAPH" = _____

_____

_____

_____

Transmission of energy in the universe is in the form of "waves"
(Light waves, heat waves, sound waves, etc.).

_____

_____

_____

Summary

_____

_____

_____

_____

_____

_____

_____

6. The Day/Age Theory of Creation

In this section we will examine another attempt to harmonize the Evolution theory with the Creation story in the Bible. (Genesis 1:3-5)

Intro – Review – Chronology

1. God exists _____

2. God creates the world.

    a. _____

    b. Job 38:4-7 _____

    _____

    - Hebrews 1:14 _____

    - Psalms 104:2-5 _____

    c. _____

    GAP Theory _____

    _____

I. Day/Age Theory

The Day/Age Theory tries to fit Evolution and Creation into one piece.

_____

_____

_____

Problems with Day/Age Theory

1. Order doesn't match geological table. _____

_____

_____

2. Day/Age Theory has _____ before _____.

_____

_____

3. Grammar supports <u>days</u> not <u>ages</u>. _____

_____

    "YOM" _____

    _____

    No need to add extra meaning to the word, let it say what it says.

II. Genesis 1:3-5

1. Light (elements for light) are created. _____

_____

_____

2. The Tri-une nature of God revealed. _____

_____

_____

3. The day and night cycle is established. _____

_____

    A. _____

    B. _____

    C. _____

Summary

1. God creates _____

_____

2. He also creates _____

_____

3. He energizes _____

_____

4. He creates the basis for _____

_____

5. He sets in motion _____

_____

7. Day #2 and #3

The lesson describes the creation of the "heavens" and the peculiar atmosphere that existed in the pre-flood era. (Genesis 1:6-10)

Intro – Review of angels:

1. _____

2. _____

3. _____

    Review - Day #1:

    A. _____

    B. _____

    C. _____

    D. _____

    "YOM" = _____

_____

I. Day #2 – Genesis 1:6-8

_____

_____

    A. Jeremiah 4:25 _____

_____

    B. Isaiah 13:10 _____

_____

    C. Hebrews 9:24 _____

_____

_____

"Firmament" = _____

_____

_____

Pre-Flood environment included:

1. Liquid _____
   _____

2. Gaseous _____
   _____

3. Water _____
   _____

4. The water canopy would give the pre-flood world a special environment with special features.

   A. It would maintain _____
       _____
       _____

   B. It would have uniform _____
       _____
       _____

   C. No rain _____
       _____
       _____

   D. Proper temperature _____
       _____
       _____

   E. Canopy would act _____
       _____
       _____

   F. Modern biomedical research _____
       _____
       _____

5. Genesis 7:11 _____
   _____

6. These events explain the changes in the weather and ecology of the earth.

- o Different _____

  _____

  _____

- o Wild _____

  _____

  _____

- o Problems with _____

  _____

  _____

- o Dry _____

  _____

  _____

- o Development of _____

  _____

  _____

- o Shortened _____

  _____

  _____

Day #2 = _____

_____

II. Day #3 – Genesis 1:9-10

_____

_____

_____

_____

There is order in how God divides the elements to form creation:

1. Light from _____

_____

_____

2. Waters above from _____

_____

_____

3. Dry land from _____

_____

_____

III. Lessons from these Passages

1. God knows _____

_____

_____

2. It's ok to pray _____

_____

_____

3. Why doubt _____?

_____

_____

8. Day #3 and #4

We continue to examine the process of creation and the elements God brings into being on day number 3 and 4. (Genesis 1:11-19)

Intro – Review

Day #1 _____

Day #2 _____

Day #3 _____

I. Day #3 – Continued

Genesis 1:11-13 _____

_____

Genesis mentions three orders of plant life:

A. Vegetation _____

_____

B. Plants / herbs _____

_____

C. Trees / fruit trees _____

_____

Seed and Kind _____

_____

Fully Mature Creation _____

_____

II. Day #4

Genesis 1:14-19 _____

_____

How to explain "Light Years"? _____

_____

_____

Hittites – Genesis 23:10 _____
_____

Features of various "lights":

- Sun and Moon light givers _____
_____

- Sun and Moon emphasized _____
_____

- Stars locked in place _____
_____

Heavenly bodies serve various purposes:

A. Day/Night _____
_____

B. Glorify God – Psalm 19:1-2 _____
_____

C. Define Seasons – Psalm 104:19 _____
_____

D. Give signs to men

  o Joshua – Joshua 10:12-13 _____
_____

  o Jesus – Matthew 2:1-2 _____
_____

Summary

Day 1 _____
Day 2 _____
Day 3 _____
Day 4 _____

9. Day #5

This lesson reviews God's creation activity on day #5. The class also provides a quiz over the material covered so far. (Genesis 1:20-25)

Intro – Review

Day #1 _____

Day #2 _____

Day #3 _____

Day #4 _____

I. Day #5

Genesis 1:20-23 _____

_____

_____

Notes on 1:20-23

Evolution says _____

_____

Creation says _____

_____

First time the term "life/soul" appears _____

_____

Specific animals are mentioned _____

_____

Created ready to produce _____

_____

God blesses His creation _____

_____

_____

_____

Genesis contradicts evolution.

Genesis	Evolution

II. Day #6

Genesis 1:24-25 _____

_____

_____

Land Animals Created

- Cattle _____

_____

- Wild beast _____

_____

- Creeping things _____

_____

Notes

1. Genesis vs. Evolution _____

_____

2. Dinosaurs and Man _____

_____

3. No "Survival of the Fittest" _____

_____

4. All of these creatures have souls or consciousness _____

_____

_____

_____

Genesis #9 - Review Quiz

1. Genesis is important because it is the book
   that contains the _____ of everything.

2. Genesis explains the beginnings of 14 basic things. Name 13 of these.

   1. U _____
   2. S _____ S _____
   3. A _____ H _____
   4. L _____
   5. M _____
   6. M _____
   7. E _____
   8. L _____
   9. G _____
   10. C _____
   11. N _____
   12. R _____
   13. C _____ P _____

3. Match the words:

   Author   Genesis Written

   Higher Critic   Genesis 1-11; 12-50

   1500 B.C.   Moses

   Compiler/Editor   Confirms inspiration

   Overview Division   4-7 century B.C.

   Jesus   Dr. Gluezk

                          God

4. Man "forms" or "fashions" but only God _____.

5. List in order the three first things God created.

   _____   _____   _____

6. Circle the correct answer:

   A. The earth is how old?

      3000 years / 5-10,000 years / 1 million + years

   B. Evolutionists believe that the earth is:

      billions of years old / fairly young / eternal

   C. Geologists can <u>accurately</u> date a fossil to:

      65,000 years / 3 million years / any age

   D. True or False:

   - Something comes from nothing.   T   F
   - Evolutionary theory matches geological fact.   T   F
   - They have found some "missing links."   T   F
   - Complex forms are universal.   T   F
   - Most "dating" methods point to a young earth.   T   F
   - The Gap Theory says that there are only 24 hours in one "creation" day. T   F
   - The "day age" theory says that each day in creation equals an age of   T   F
     evolution.
   - God created matter and energized it on the same day.   T   F
   - Elements for light and the dark light cycle were created on the first day. T   F
   - The word "YOM" means creation.   T   F

7. Fill in the blanks.

- The term "heaven" could mean the atmosphere, _____ or God's throne.
- The "waters above" is a reference to a _____ _____ above the atmosphere.
- On the third day God separated the _____ from the _____.
- Heavenly bodies have special purposes; name two:

  _____

  _____

- Unlike fish, birds and animals, vegetation and matter have no _____.
- Dinosaurs were created at the same time as _____.

Bonus Question (5 POINTS):

Genesis 1:1 has been referred to as the "foundational" verse in the Bible. Why?

_____

_____

_____

_____

10. The Creation of Man

This lesson examines the Divine Council and the similarities between the natures of God and man. (Genesis 1:26-31)

Intro – Review

- Creation of _____
- Creation of _____

I. Creation of Man – Genesis 1:26-27

_____

_____

The Divine Council

Genesis 1:26a _____

_____

_____

I Peter 1:20 _____

_____

_____

Psalm 110:1; Isaiah 48:16; John 17:24 _____

_____

_____

Info About God

1. God _____

_____

_____

2. God _____

_____

_____

3. The creation _____

_____

_____

Info About Man

1. The term "man" _____

_____

_____

2. The term "Adam" _____

_____

_____

3. Adam's triune nature:

A. Has a _____

_____

B. Has _____

_____

C. Possess _____

_____

Ecclesiastes 3:21 _____

_____

_____

Ephesians 1:9 _____

_____

_____

II. Man's Position

Genesis 1:26b _____

_____

_____

_____

III. The Act of Creation

Genesis 1:27 _____

_____

_____

_____

IV. God's Charge to Man

Two unknown worlds.

    A. _____

    B. _____

Genesis 1:28-31 _____

_____

_____

_____

    1. Only 1 _____ and 1 _____

_____

_____

    2. Fill the _____

_____

_____

3. Subdue and have _____

   _____

   _____

   _____

4. They ate no _____

   _____

   _____

   _____

5. God sees that all was _____ _____

   _____

   _____

   _____

Summary

_____

_____

_____

_____

_____

_____

_____

11. God's Rest and Man's Creation

This lesson continues to describe in greater detail the creation of human beings as well as the nature of the "rest" God takes after His creative activity. (Genesis 2:1-7)

Intro – Review three acts of creation:

- Creation of _____
- Creation of _____
- Creation of _____

I. Day of Rest – 2:1-3

Genesis 2:1 _____

_____

Genesis 2:2 _____

_____

Genesis 2:3 _____

_____

II. Adam's Perspective

Generational Divisions:

Genesis 1:1 – 2:4 _____

_____

Genesis 2:4 – 5:1 _____

_____

Genesis 5:1 – 6:9 _____

_____

Genesis 6:9 – 10:1 _____

_____

Genesis 10:1 – 11:10 _____

_____

Genesis 11:10 – 11:27 _____

_____

Genesis 11:27 – 25:29 _____

_____

Genesis 25:29 – 37:2 _____

_____

Genesis 37:2 – Exodus 1:1 _____

_____

Genesis 2:4 _____

_____

Genesis 5:1 _____

_____

III. Pre-Sin Environment

Genesis 2:5-6 _____

_____

IV. The Creation of Man – In Detail

Genesis 2:7 _____

_____

Formed _____

_____

Elements _____

_____

Energized _____

_____

God – Like _____

_____

First and Only _____

_____

12. The Moral Choice

This lesson will examine how God created the impulse in man that is his will as well as his sense of need. (Genesis 2:8-20)

Intro – Review – Genesis 1:1-2:7

1. _____
2. _____
3. _____
4. _____

I. The Garden – 2:8-14

Vs. 8 _____

_____

Vs. 9 _____

_____

Vs. 10-14 _____

_____

- II Peter 3:6 _____

_____

II. The Moral Choice – vs. 15-17

Man is fully equipped. _____

_____

An environment where man can co-exist with God. ___

_____

The answer is a "Moral" realm. _____

_____

Vs. 16-17 _____

_____

_____

God's command does several things:

1. Activates _____

_____

2. Puts man's _____

_____

3. Makes possible _____

_____

III. Man and the Animals – vs. 18-20

_____

_____

Vs. 18 _____

_____

"HELPMEET" _____

_____

Vs. 19-20 _____

_____

Adam's review of the animals suggests:

1. He was created _____

_____

2. He was intelligent _____

_____

3. He learned:

   - _____

   _____

   - _____

   _____

   - _____

   _____

13. The Creation of Woman

In this section the writer of Genesis not only describes the unique creation of woman but also sets forth God's foundational principles for marriage and the family unit. (Genesis 2:21-25)

Intro – Review

1. God initiates _____

   Moral choice gives man:

   1. Superiority over _____

   2. Can relate to _____

   3. Freedom to _____

2. God instructs _____

3. God leads _____

   _____

I. The Creation of Woman – Genesis 2:21-22

1. The "sleep of Adam" _____

   _____

2. The word "Rib" _____

   _____

3. God forms woman _____

   _____

4. God brings woman to man _____

   _____

II. The Family – Genesis 2:23-25

The first social unit is the family.

_____

_____

Vs. 23 _____

_____

Adam acknowledges that Eve is _____

_____

Vs. 24 _____

_____

1. Activates _____ a family is made up of _____

_____

_____

      Families are formed when _____

_____

2. Basic Ingredients _____

_____

      ■ Intimacy _____

               _____

      ■ Exclusivity _____

               _____

      ■ Longevity_____

               _____

      Vs. 25 _____

_____

How did Adam and Eve Marry?

    • Knowledge _____

_____

    • Covenant _____

_____

    • Confirmation _____

_____

They were not ashamed. _____

_____

_____

14. The First Appearance of Satan in the Bible

This lesson explains the first glimpse of Satan in the physical world and examines information about this spiritual being from various Bible writers. (Genesis 3:1)

Intro – The problem of failure and death has been much discussed by philosophers and theologians.

_____

Some answers from human thinking:

Atheism _____

Dualism _____

Materialism _____

Romans 5:12 _____

_____

I. Satan

Genesis 3:1a _____

_____

Isaiah 14:12-15 _____

_____

Ezekiel 28:12-19 _____

_____

Satan was _____ vs. 13b

Satan was _____ vs. 12-13

Satan was _____ vs. 12-13

Satan served _____.

Satan was _____ vs. 15

Satan's sin _____ vs. 15

Satan's source _____ vs. 17a

Satan tried to _____ Jude 6

Satan's destruction was _____ vs. 17-19

Satan no longer _____

II. Satan and the Serpent – 3:1b

Why and how a serpent's body? _____

_____

_____

Satan was fallen _____

_____

_____

Satan is naturally _____

_____

_____

I John 4:4 _____

_____

_____

Who was doing the talking?

_____

_____

_____

Summary

If Satan possessed the snake...

_____

_____

If Satan guided the snake...

_____

_____

Hollywood's take.

_____

_____

_____

15. Eve's 5 Mistakes

This lesson reviews the mistakes Eve made which led her to commit the first sin in human history. (Genesis 3:1-6)

Intro – Satan's first appearance _____

_____

Two Trees:

    A. Tree of _____

    B. Tree of _____

I. Eve's 5 Mistakes – Genesis 3:1b-6

_____

Mistake #1 – She _____.

_____

_____

      Genesis 3:2a _____

      _____

Mistake #2 – She _____.

_____

_____

      Genesis 3:4-6a _____

      _____

      _____

      Satan accuses God of:

      _____ and _____

      _____

Mistake #3 – She _____.

_____

_____

In considering the offer she was opening herself up for temptation at three levels:

1. Physical _____

   _____

2. Emotional _____

   _____

3. Spiritual _____

   _____

John 2:16 _____

_____

_____

Luke 4:1-12 – Jesus' temptation was similar.

Physical _____

Emotional _____

Spiritual _____

What should Eve have done?

A. Stand _____ Ephesians 6:11

   _____

   _____

B. Run _____ Timothy 2:22

   _____

   _____

Ecclesiastes 9:4 _____

_____

_____

Eve said to herself _____ _____.

_____

_____

Mistake #4 – She _____.

_____

_____

Genesis 3:6b _____

_____

_____

The simple command was "_____ _____ _____ _____."

_____

_____

Mistake #5 – She _____.

_____

_____

Genesis 3:6c _____

_____

_____

_____

The 5 Stages of Temptation

1. Failure to _____

_____

_____

_____

2. Compromising _____

_____

_____

_____

3. Considering _____

_____

_____

_____

4. Consent _____

_____

_____

5. Start _____

_____

_____

_____

16. The Judgment

After Adam and Eve's sin the Bible describes the judgement imposed on Satan, Eve and Adam. (Genesis 3:2-16)

Intro – Review – Eve's 5 Mistakes

Mistake #1 – Failure _____.

Mistake #2 – Compromising _____.

Mistake #3 – Considering _____.

Mistake #4 – _____ to sin.

Mistake #5 – Start _____.

I. Consequences of Sin

_____

_____

1. _____ - vs. 7a

_____

_____

2. _____ - vs. 7b

_____

_____

3. _____ - vs. 8-10

_____

_____

4. _____ - vs. 11-13

_____

_____

5. _____ - vs. 14-21

_____

_____

A. Satan is Judged – vs. 14-15

_____

_____

_____

Men have _____.

The seed of woman is _____.

The seed of Satan is _____.

B. Eve is Judged – vs. 16

_____

_____

_____

Before sin, _____ would be without pain.

_____

_____

Before sin Adam and Eve enjoyed _____ over creation.

_____

_____

After sin...

_____

_____

God shows His mercy in Judgment.

_____

_____

17. Paradise Lost

In this lesson God describes the consequences of sin on Adam, Eve, and the creation. (Genesis 3:17-24)

Intro – 5 consequences of sin:

1. _____

2. _____

3. _____

4. _____

5. _____

I. Judgment of Man

Genesis 3:17-19 _____

_____

_____

Once sin enters the world, God removes His presence and the cycle of deterioration begins.

_____

_____

This concept of universal deterioration has been scientifically formulated for over 100 years

(Carnot, Clausius, Kelvin, and others) _____

_____

_____

It's called the Second Law of Thermodynamics and states that _____

_____

_____

The "cursing" of the ground in Genesis 3:17 is the reverse of _____

_____

_____

Better suffering and death than _____

_____

_____

The result of the "curse":

1. Sorrow _____
_____

2. Pain and Suffering _____
_____

3. Hard Work _____
_____

4. Death _____
_____

      Curse on Adam / Curse on Jesus

      Isaiah 53:3 _____

      Mark 15:17 _____

      Luke 22:44 _____

      Psalm 22:15 _____

II. Paradise Lost

Genesis 3:20 _____
_____

Adam re-names the woman which will signify:

1. Life _____
_____

2. Faith _____
_____

3. Renewal _____
_____

      Genesis 3:21 _____

      Genesis 3:22 _____

      Genesis 3:23-24 _____

      Revelation 2:7 _____
_____

18. Cain and Abel

This lesson explores the series of events leading up to the first murder. (Genesis 4:1-8)

Intro – The Fall of Man – Review

1. The Command _____

   _____

2. The Disobedience _____

   _____

3. The Salvation _____

   _____

I. Murder of Abel

Adam and Eve believe and respond to God's promise.

_____

_____

Vs. 1 _____

_____

Vs. 2 _____

_____

Occupations:

Abel – Shepherd _____

Cain – Farmer _____

_____

_____

Genesis 1:29; 2:16; 3:19 _____

_____

Population Statistics _____

_____

_____

Vs. 3-5 – Various interpretations:

1. _____

2. _____

3. _____

Biblical references to Abel:

1. Matthew 23:35_____

2. Luke 11:49-51 _____

3. Hebrews 11:4 _____

Cain's reaction _____
_____

Vs. 6-7 – God warns Cain:

1. Face _____ _____.
_____

2. Acknowledge _____.
_____

    I John 3:12 _____
_____

3. Deal _____ _____.
_____

    Vs. 8 – What did Cain and Abel argue about? _____
_____

II. Final Lessons

1. _____
_____

2. _____
_____

3. _____
_____

19. The Punishment of Cain

This passage looks at the result of Cain's sin and the punishment meted out to him by God. (Genesis 4:9-24)

Intro – The 4 angles of the Genesis story.

1. Close-Up _____

2. Society _____

3. Seed of Promise _____

4. War of the "Seeds" _____

I. Cain's Judgment – 4:9-15

Vs. 9 _____

_____

Cain's response _____

_____

_____

Vs. 10 _____

_____

Vs. 11-12 – The consequences of sin in Cain's life:

    a. The land _____

       _____

    b. Wandering _____

       _____

         Vs. 13 _____

         Vs. 14 _____

    c. No communion with the Lord _____

       _____

    d. The "Mark" _____

       _____

         Vs. 15 _____

       _____

II. The Way of Cain

Vs. 16 _____

Vs. 17 _____

Vs. 18 _____

Vs. 19 – Lamech _____

Vs. 20-22 _____

    1. JABAL _____

    2. JUBAL _____

    3. TUBAL-CAIN _____

Society's development through Cain:

    A. Urban life _____

    _____

    B. Nomadic life _____

    _____

    C. Cattle raising _____

    _____

    D. Metal working _____

    _____

    E. Musical instruments _____

    _____

    F. Polygamy _____

    _____

    G. Metallic weapons _____

    _____

    H. Writing and Art _____

    _____

        Vs. 23-24 _____

    _____

        1. _____

        2. _____

20. Seed of Promise

In this section of Genesis, the author identifies and traces the lineage of those people who will eventually deliver the Seed of Promise to mankind. (Genesis 4:25-5:32)

Intro – The 4 Views

1. Close-Up _____

_____

_____

2. Social _____

_____

_____

3. Seed of Promise _____

_____

_____

4. War of the "Seeds" _____

_____

_____

I. Seed of Promise

1. The story in Genesis now shifts its focus to the image of the "Seed of Promise." _____

_____

_____

Vs. 25 _____

_____

_____

Vs. 26 _____

_____

_____

II. Generations of Adam

1. Divisions of Genesis
   A. Creation – 1-11
   B. Chosen People – 12-50
2. Generational Divisions
   A. Generation of _____ and _____ 1:1 – 2:4
   B. Generation of _____ 2:4 – 5:1
   C. Generation of _____ 5:1 – 6:9
   D. Generation of Sons of _____ 6:9 – 10:1
   E. Generation of Sons of _____ 10:1 – 11:10
   F. Generation of _____ 11:10 – 11:27
   G. Generation of _____ 11:27 – 25:29
   H. Generation of _____ 25:29 – 37:2
   I. Generation of _____ 37:2 – Ex. 1:1

Genesis 5:1a _____

_____

_____

Vs. 1b-2 _____

_____

_____

_____

Vs. 3-5 _____

_____

_____

_____

Vs. 6-32 _____

_____

_____

_____

Antediluvian Patriarchs

Patriarch	Meaning	Birth	Death
Adam		1	
Seth		130	
Enosh		235	
Cainan		325	
Mahlaleel		395	
Zared		460	
Enoch		622	
Methuselah		687	
Lamech		874	
Noah		1056	

FAQs About Patriarchs:

1. Patriarchs _____
   _____
   _____

2. Adam _____
   _____
   _____

3. Methuselah _____
   _____
   _____

4. Lamech _____
   _____
   _____

Lessons

A. God is _____.

_____

_____

_____

_____

B. God's plan will _____.

_____

_____

_____

_____

21. The Times of Noah

This lesson looks at the condition of the antediluvian world that Noah lived in and examines the information the Bible gives us about this Old Testament Patriarch. (Genesis 6:1-13)

Intro – Review

    1. Adam's Record _____

_____

    2. Noah's Summary _____

_____

I. Noah – Genesis 6:1

Matthew 24:37-39 _____

_____

Genesis 6:1-4 _____

_____

    1. Angels and Women _____

    2. Cain and Seth's Descendants _____

    3. Cain and Demons _____

A. The condition of the world was wicked _____

_____

Genesis 6:5-6 _____

_____

B. More details about the Antediluvian world:

    1. Preoccupation with_____ Luke 17:26-27

_____

    2. Satanic _____ Genesis 6:2

    3. General _____ Hebrews 11:7

    4. Ungodly_____ Jude 14-15

    5. Widespread_____ Genesis 6:11-13

Genesis 6:7 _____

_____

Genesis 6:8 _____

_____

Profile of Noah

Obedient _____

_____

(Genesis 6:22; 7:5; 7:9; 7:16)

- One _____ (Genesis 7:13)
- Preacher _____ (II Peter 2:5)
- Ministry was a _____ (Hebrews 11:7)
- Master _____ (Ark)
- Offered _____ (Genesis 8:20; 9:20)
- Farmer _____ (Genesis 9:24)
- Considered _____ (Genesis 9:6)

Genesis 6:9-10 _____

_____

Genesis 6:11-13 _____

_____

Lessons

1. Perseverance not _____

_____

2. We don't have _____

_____

3. God can _____ us _____.

_____

_____

_____

22. The Building of the Ark

This lesson contains many details concerning the dimensions and building of the Ark as well as its use as a "type" for the church. (Genesis 6:14-22)

Intro – God's judgment has been pronounced. _____

_____

I. The Building of the Ark

Genesis 4:14-16 _____

_____

Statistics

1. Ark _____

_____

2. Measurements _____

_____

3. No Tipping Over _____

_____

4. 1.4 Million Cubic Feet _____

_____

5. Multi Storied _____

_____

6. Construction Materials _____

_____

7. Windows and Doors _____

_____

II. God's Judgment and Promises

Vs. 17_____

_____

1. God brings _____

_____

2. "Flood of Waters"

- Mabbul Mayim _____

- Kata Clusmos _____

3. The flood will _____

_____

Vs. 18 _____

_____

Agreement   _____

_____

Covenant   _____

_____

Vs. 19-21 _____

Vs. 22 – Noah enters into a covenant with God. _____

Lessons

1. The Ark is a "type" for the church.

    A. One ark _____

    B. Safety in ark _____

    C. One way into ark _____

    D. Alive through water in the ark _____

    E. Ark carries to the next life _____

    F. Only believers in the ark _____

    G. Ark was mocked _____

    H. Ark built by believers _____

    I. God provided for the ark _____

    J. Ark necessary _____

2. You need to be in and stay in _____.

_____

23. Flood Details

In this lesson, we get a "close-up" view of the final preparations for the impending flood and physical details concerning the cause and destructive power of this cataclysmic event. (Genesis 7:1-24)

Intro – Review

- All invited into the ark _____
- All invited into the church _____
- God's covenant with Noah: _____

I. God Breaks His Silence – 7:1-10

Vs. 1 _____

_____

God brings the animas to the ark but He _____ Noah to enter.

_____

Vs. 2-3 – Division of animals.

- Clean/Unclean _____

_____

- Domestic/Wild _____

_____

Vs. 4-5 _____

_____

KOL – YEYUM = _____

Everything would be destroyed _____

_____ _____

Vs. 6-9 _____

_____

End of ANDIDELOVIAN Age _____

_____

120 Years = 1000 Years _____

_____

II. The Flood

Vs. 10-11a _____

Vs. 11b-12 _____

Fountains of the great deep _____
_____

Windows of heaven _____
_____

Trigger that caused flood:

- Theological   = _____

- Realistically   = _____

- Naturally   = _____

Vs. 13-16 _____
_____

The flood is a "worldwide" catastrophe. _____
_____

Vs. 17-18 _____

Vs. 19-20 _____

Vs. 21-23 – The Bible specifically says that <u>everything</u> was destroyed. _____
_____

Vs. 24 _____
_____

Lessons

1. God keeps _____
_____

2. God requires _____
_____

3. God is _____
_____

24. Effects of the Great Flood

The book of Genesis records the extent of the damage caused by the worldwide flood and the changes that resulted from this cataclysmic event. (Genesis 8:1-9:6)

Intro – Church/Ark – Judgment/Flood _____

_____

I. Results of the Flood – 8:1-14

Vs. 1-2 _____

_____

God stopped the flood:

o   Caused a great _____

o   Stopped the _____

o   Closed the _____

Vs. 3 – Water recedes, land appears. _____

_____

Vs. 4 _____

_____

Vs. 5-12   - In the ark _____days

                    - It took the earth _____ months to dry.

Vs. 13-14 – Noah made sure the earth was dry before he opened it. _____

_____

Physical changes to the earth <u>after</u> a great world-wide flood.

1. Oceans _____

2. Less _____

3. Thermal vapor barrier now lessened. What happens next? _____

_____

4. Rise of mountains, which, in effect, makes much land uninhabitable. _____

_____

5. Movement of the crust creates greater movement. _____

6. Fossil records everywhere misinterpreted by translators. _____

_____

II. God and Noah after the Flood

Vs. 15-19 _____

_____

- Dr. Andrew Woods, "The Center of the Earth" _____
- Some animals become extinct after the flood. _____

_____

Vs. 20 _____

_____

Vs. 21-22 – God responds to Noah's prayer by promising two things:

1. No curse
2. New environment will be able to sustain man

_____

_____

III. Establishment of Human Government – Genesis 9:1-7

Vs. 1-2 _____

Vs. 3-4 _____

No Blood!

- Physically dangerous
- Theologically one didn't eat blood, he offered to God <u>first.</u>
- Avoid pagan practices.

Vs. 5-6 _____

_____

Death Penalty

- Both Old/New Testament support, encourage its use.
- Encourages mercy for guilty

25. The Rainbow Covenant

This lesson explains the promises made by God to Noah concerning the survival of his family and Noah's prophecy about the future of each of his sons and their descendants. (Genesis 9:7-29)

Intro – Review

1. The physical world has changed. _____

2. The social world has changed. _____

3. The spiritual world has changed. _____

      Genesis 9:7 _____

      Genesis 8:22 _____

I. The Rainbow Covenant – 9:8-29

God makes a covenant with Noah. _____

_____

Genesis 9:8-10 _____

_____

Genesis 9:11-17 _____

_____

II. Sons of Noah

There are a variety of ways to classify the different "races" in the world. _____

_____

9:18-19 _____

9:20-23 _____

_____

Here we see the reactions of the three sons:

      Ham _____

_____

      Shem/Japheth _____

_____

Similarities between Adam and Noah.

ADAM	NOAH
1. _____	1. _____
2. _____	2. _____
3. _____	3. _____
4. _____	4. _____
5. _____	5. _____
6. _____	6. _____
7. _____	7. _____

Genesis 9:24-27 _____

_____

HAM - Ham will have a position of service to his brothers, not slavery _____

_____

Ham's Descendants

- Original explorers _____
- First cultivators _____
- Developed tools _____
- Developed weaving _____
- Discovered medicines _____
- Invented basic math _____
- Banking, postal systems _____
- Paper, ink _____

Shem's Descendants

- Semitic peoples – Abraham _____
- Relationship and knowledge of God _____

Japheth's Descendants

- Would be enlarged _____
  _____

- Dwell in tents _____
  _____

- Would be served by Ham _____
  _____

These three are the source of streams of nations, and how each has developed.

A. Semites _____
  _____
  _____

B. Jephites _____
  _____
  _____

C. Hamites _____
  _____
  _____

9:28-29 _____
_____
_____
_____

26. The Table and the Tower

Lesson #26 looks at two fascinating source events that explain the origins of all the different nations and languages in the world today.
(Genesis 10:1-11:32)

Intro – Review

Condition of Post-Diluvian world

- Environment _____

- Society _____

- Spiritual Promise _____

Noah's Prophecies

- Ham _____

- Shem _____

- Japheth _____

I. Table of Nations – Genesis 10

Genesis 10:1-5 _____

_____

_____

Genesis 10:6-20 _____

_____

_____

God's commands:

1. To _____

2. To _____

3. To _____

Nimrod and Rebellion _____

_____

_____

Genesis 10:21-32 _____

_____

II. Tower of Babel

Genesis 11:1 _____

_____

_____

Genesis 11:2 _____

_____

_____

Genesis 11:3-4 _____

_____

_____

God's purpose challenged.

- They want _____

  _____

- They begin _____

  _____

- The new philosophy is _____

  _____

  _____

Genesis 11:5-6 _____

_____

_____

Genesis 11:7-9 _____

_____

_____

A smaller circle of reproduction caused _____

_____

_____

The "Miracle" of Tongues

Adam _____

_____

_____

Babel _____

_____

_____

Pentecost _____

_____

_____

Genesis 11:10-26 _____

_____

_____

Genesis 11:27-32 – Terah's record ends. _____

_____

_____

Bonus Material – Ziggurats

27. Abraham: Father of a Nation

With the beginning of chapter twelve, the book of Genesis focuses once again on one specific individual. This time the writers will detail the life of Abraham who was to become the father of the Jewish nation and how the Seed of Promise was kept alive through him. (Genesis 12:1-20)

Intro – Review

- Japheth _____
- Ham _____
- Shem _____
- Terah begins to record _____
    - Haran _____
    - Nahor _____
    - Abram _____

I. Abraham – The Call – 12:1-9

_____

_____

God makes promises to Abram:

- He will become _____

  _____

- He himself will be _____

  _____

- He will bless _____

  _____

- He will _____

  _____

- The entire world will be_____ by _____.

  _____

- The land would _____

  _____

II. Abraham in Egypt – 12:10-20

Vs. 10_____

_____

The problem:

1. God told him to _____

2. God promised _____

3. Egypt was _____

_____

_____

Vs. 11-13 _____

_____

Vs. 14-16 _____

_____

Vs. 17-20 _____

_____

Pharaoh rebukes Abraham:

- Upset at what Abraham has done.

- His rebuke is harsh because:

_____

_____

_____

Lessons

1. It's about _____ not _____.

_____

2. A promise is a _____.

_____

_____

3. You can't _____ a faith that you _____ _____.

_____

28. Abraham and Lot

This lesson reviews the relationship between Abraham and his nephew Lot as well as the godly wisdom the family leader used to resolve a serious dispute. (Genesis 13:1-18)

Intro – Review

Origins in Genesis:

- _____

- _____

Abraham's calling:

A. _____

B. _____

C. _____

I. Lot's Choice – Chapter 13

A. Abram's Return – Genesis 13:1-4 _____

_____

B. Abram's Decision – Genesis 13:5-13 _____

_____

Vs. 5-7 _____

_____

Vs. 8-13 – Note how Abram solves the problem:

    1. Describes _____

_____

    2. Proposes _____

_____

    3. Allows _____

_____

C. Lot's Decision

_____

_____

Lot served himself:

1. _____

2. _____

3. _____

4. _____

D. God Renames His Promise – Genesis 13:14-18_____

_____

God renews and expands His promise:

1. All can't _____

_____

2. Head of nation _____

_____

E. Abram's History _____

_____

Lessons

1. God will _____

_____

2. Sin always _____

_____

3. God's Word _____

_____

_____

_____

"We shouldn't wait for _____ to _____

our _____, we should say, "The _____ says

this and I _____ it."

29. Melchizedek: A 'Type' for Christ

This lesson introduces the fascinating figure of Melchizedek, one of the earliest types or previews for Christ in the Bible. (Genesis 14:1-24)

Intro – Review Abraham

- Descendant of _____
- From _____
- Father was _____
- Father died in _____
- Went to _____
- Told a _____ to Pharaoh
- Nephew was _____

Promises from God

- Great _____
- Great _____
- Bless _____
- Protection _____

- Worldwide _____
- Multiply _____
- Land _____

I. Northeastern Kings

The War – Genesis 14:1-12

_____

_____

The Rescue – 14:13-16

_____

_____

"Hebrew" meant several things:

A. Beyond _____

_____

B. Descendants of _____

_____

C. A moving tribe _____

_____

_____

Melchizedek – 14:17-20

_____

_____

Vs. 17 _____

_____

Vs. 18 _____

_____

Vs. 19 _____

_____

Vs. 20 _____

_____

_____

The appearance of Melchizedek _____

_____

_____

He is a "type" _____

_____

God uses a Billboard Method to preview events and people in the future:

1. He will promise or warn _____

_____

_____

2. He will send a prophet _____

_____

_____

3. He will provide a "type" _____
_____
_____

Examples of Types

Ark _____   Promised Land _____

Sacrifice _____   Elijah _____

Jews _____

_____
_____

Melchizedek _____
_____
_____

Hebrews 7:1-2 _____
_____
_____

Hebrews 7:3 _____
_____
_____

Hebrews 7:4-5 _____
_____
_____
_____

The King of Sodom – Genesis 14:21-24

_____

_____

_____

Lessons

1. Flee from _____

_____

_____

_____

_____

2. Destroy not _____

_____

_____

_____

_____

3. God is a patient _____

_____

_____

_____

_____

30. The Gospel in the Old Testament

In this section of Genesis God reveals the core principle of the Gospel to Abraham, salvation by a process of faith. (Genesis 15:1-21)

Intro – Review Abraham's Life _____

_____

I. The Promise Reviewed – Chapter 15

Vs. 1 _____

First time for:

1. Word of _____

2. Word as _____

3. "I AM" passages _____

4. "Fear not" passages _____

   _____

Comparison of Adam and Abraham:

Adam	Abraham
• _____	• _____
• _____	• _____
• _____	• _____

Vs. 2-6 _____

_____

- Believe _____

  _____

- Counted _____

  _____

- Righteousness _____

  _____

- Melchizedek was a _____ for _____

- Abraham is a _____ for _____

- God imputed righteousness on Abraham because _____
_____

- God imputes righteousness upon us because _____
_____

Vs. 7-21 _____
_____

Features of the vision:

1. _____
_____

2. _____
_____

3. _____
_____

4. _____
_____

5. _____
_____

God also gives a guarantee of our promise. _____
_____

Lessons

1. We are saved _____
_____

2. We continue to be saved _____
_____

3. We will succeed by _____
_____

31. Sarai and Hagar's Conflict / Abram and Circumcision

This lesson looks at the very source of the Jewish/Arab conflict as well as the distinguishing mark given to Abraham and all his male descendants... circumcision. (Genesis 16:1-17:27)

Intro – Abram believed and God _____ it to him as _____

Key Ideas:

1. Saved because _____

2. Holy because we _____

3. Faith is a _____ relationship.

I. Sarai's Solution – 16:1-4

Vs. 1-4 _____

_____

She fell short of God's will in two ways:

1. She violated the _____

_____

2. She took charge of _____

_____

II. Hagar's Promise – 16:5-16

Vs. 5-6 _____

Vs. 7-9 _____

Vs. 10-12 _____

Vs. 13-14 _____

_____

- Information on **Ishmael** _____

_____

Vs. 15-16 _____

_____

_____

III. Covenant Reviewed – 17:1-8

_____

_____

IV. Covenant Confirmed – 17:9-14

Circumcision represented many things:

    A. Sign of Seed _____

        _____

    B. Enclosure of God's will _____

        _____

    C. Sign of Faith _____

        _____

    D. Sign of Sanctification _____

        _____

V. Name Change – 17:15-27

_____

_____

Lessons

    1. God's Way _____

        _____

        _____

    2. Circumcision is a _____

        _____

        _____

    3. Wait _____

        _____

        _____

32. Lot's Poor Choices

In this lesson, we see the very real consequences of Lot's choices concerning where he chose to live with his family after separating from Abraham. (Genesis 18:1-19:38)

Intro – We have covered two core ideas:

1. We are saved _____
2. Faith in God is expressed _____
    _____

Circumcision

- Sign of _____
- Enclosure _____
- Sign of _____
- Signs of _____

Circumcision and Baptism

Circumcision was a _____ for baptism.

_____

I. The Visit to Abram – 18:1-22

_____

Vs. 12 _____

Vs. 13-15 _____

_____

II. Abram's Intercession – 18:23-33

1. First time _____
    _____

2. Acknowledges that God is _____
    _____

3. Abram's prayer _____
    _____
    _____

III. Lot at the Gates of Sodom – 19:1-3

Vs.1 _____

_____

Vs. 2-3 _____

_____

Vs. 4-11 _____

_____

Lot offers his own daughters to the mob _____

_____

Vs. 12-14 _____

_____

Vs. 15-23 _____

_____

Vs. 24-29 _____

_____

What destroyed Sodom could have been:

1. _____

2. _____

3. _____

Vs. 30-38 _____

Lessons

1. Be _____

_____

2. Nothing is too _____

_____

3. Mercy **and** Justice _____

_____

4. Don't _____

_____

33. The Source of Islam

In chapters 20 and 21 of Genesis, we read about Abraham's continued walk of faith and a description of the people who were the source for the religion of Islam. (Genesis 20:1-21:34)

Intro – Abraham's Faith _____

_____

Lot's Faith _____

_____

_____

I. Failure – Genesis 20:1-18

Abraham journeys to the land of the Philistines and meets King Abimelech.

_____

_____

God deals with Abimelech.

1. He inflicts _____

   _____

2. He prevents _____

   _____

3. He reveals _____

   _____

Abimelech deals with Abraham and Sarah.

1. He rebukes _____

   _____

2. He rebukes _____

   _____

3. He gives _____

   _____

II. The Child of Promise – 21:1-34

Vs. 1-8 – The birth of Isaac _____

_____

_____

Vs. 9-14 – Sarah sends Hagar away _____

_____

_____

Vs. 15-21 – Hagar's journey _____

_____

_____

The religion of Islam (surrender)

1. Cultural source _____

_____

_____

2. Rivalry _____

_____

_____

3. Ceremonies _____

_____

_____

- Articles of _____

_____

- Right _____

_____

- Religious _____

_____

o   Mecca _____

_____

_____

_____

o   Sarah and Hagar are _____

_____

_____

_____

A. Hagar represents _____

- Descendants _____

- Justification _____

- Jerusalem _____

- Persecute _____

- Slaves _____

B. Sarah represents _____

- Descendants _____

- Justification _____

- True Home _____

- Temple _____

- Persecution _____

- Children _____

Vs. 22-34 _____

_____

_____

Lessons

1. Never too old _____

_____

_____

_____

_____

_____

2. Mountain tops lead to _____

_____

_____

_____

_____

_____

3. His time is not _____

_____

_____

_____

_____

_____

34. Abraham's Test

This lesson leads to the climax of Abraham's journey of faith and describes the events surrounding Sarah's death. (Genesis 22:1-23:20)

Intro – Genesis introduces us to two ancient and great cultures and their sources.

HAGAR	SARAH	_____
↓	↓	_____
ISHMAEL	ISAAC	_____
↓	↓	_____
ARABS	ISRAEL	_____
↓	↓	_____
ISLAM	JUDAISM	_____
	↓	_____
	CHRISTIANITY	

I. Test of Faith – Genesis 22:1-2

Twenty years of silence between chapters 21 and 22

_____

_____

Vs. 1-2 – Two important words are used here:

1. Tempted _____

_____

2. Love _____

_____

Vs. 3-8 – Abraham leaves with Isaac to do what God has asked of him. _____

_____

Note that Abraham tells the servants that they <u>both</u> will return.

In this statement we see his great faith. _____

_____

Vs. 9-14 – In these verses we see several "types" that project ahead three important ideas:

1. _____

_____

2. _____

_____

3. _____

_____

Vs. 15-24 _____

_____

II. The Death of Sarah – 23:1-20

_____

_____

_____

III. Lessons for Today

1. Expect _____

_____

_____

2. Expect _____

_____

_____

3. Expect _____

_____

_____

35. Types in Genesis

This lesson reviews some important types or previews that are contained in Genesis and realized centuries later in the New Testament. (Genesis 24:1-67)

Intro – Abraham's sacrifice of his son, Isaac, provides us with "types" that foreshadow features of the Christian faith:

1. The Sacrifice: _____

   _____

2. Vicarious: _____

   _____

3. Faith and _____

   _____

The next chapter offers up more types fulfilled in the New Testament

I. Search for a Bride – Genesis 24:1

Finding a wife for Isaac was a critical decision.

_____

_____

Vs. 1-4 – The hand under the thigh. _____

_____

_____

Vs. 5-9 – The servant is unsure of his mission. _____

_____

_____

Vs. 6-14 – The servant's prayer. _____

_____

_____

Vs. 15-27 – The servant's prayer answered. _____

_____

_____

Vs. 28-33 – Rebekah's family. _____

_____

_____

Vs. 34-49 – The servant's request. _____

_____

_____

The servant as a type for the Holy Spirit.

- Sent _____
- Presence _____
- Declares _____
- Requires _____

Vs. 50-61 – The family's response _____

_____

_____

The Holy Spirit as type in the Old Testament

▪ Immediate decision _____

_____

_____

- New Life _____
  _____
  _____

- New Spirit _____
  _____
  _____

Vs. 62-67 – Isaac and Rebekah meet and marry. _____
_____
_____

Isaac and Rebekah as types for Christ and the church.

Isaac/Christ
- Promised
- Appeared at certain time
- Conceived miraculously
- Assigned name
- Offered as sacrifice
- Obedient unto death
- Resurrected
- Head of people

Rebekah/church
- Marriage planned
- Accomplishes purpose
- Shares glory of Son
- Found by messenger
- Leaves all
- Accompanied by messenger
- United by Son

_____
_____
_____

II. Some Basic Lessons

1. Be _____

_____

_____

_____

_____

_____

2. Character _____

_____

_____

_____

_____

_____

3. It's all about _____

_____

_____

_____

_____

_____

36. The Life of Esau and Jacob

After the death of Abraham, the promise is passed on to one of his sons but not without difficulty and division in his family. (Genesis 25:1-26:35)

Intro – Isaac and Rebekah are "types"

_____

_____

_____

I. The Death of Abraham – Genesis 25:1-4

Vs. 1-4 _____

_____

_____

Vs. 5-10 - Abraham dies at 175 years _____

_____

_____

_____

II. Transition – Genesis 25:11-18

Ishmael's Generation _____

_____

_____

Isaac's Record _____

_____

_____

_____

III. Esau and Jacob – Genesis 26:19-34

Vs. 19-23 _____

_____

_____

Vs. 24-26 _____

_____

_____

_____

_____

Vs. 27-34 – Comparing Jacob and Esau:

ESAU	JACOB
• _____	• _____
• _____	• _____
• _____	• _____
• _____	• _____
• _____	• _____

_____

_____

_____

Vs. 29-34 _____

_____

_____

_____

IV. Isaac vs. the Philistines

Genesis 26:1-5 _____

_____

God's appearance to him suggested several things:

1. A warning _____

   _____

   _____

2. An encouragement _____

   _____

   _____

3. A word of rebuke _____

   _____

   _____

   Vs. 6-11 _____

   _____

   _____

   Vs. 12-16 _____

   _____

   _____

   Vs. 17-22 _____

   _____

   _____

   Vs. 23-25 _____

   _____

   _____

Vs. 26-33 _____

_____

_____

Vs. 34-35 _____

_____

_____

Lessons

1. Be careful _____

_____

_____

_____

2. You never suffer _____

_____

_____

_____

3. A promise _____

_____

_____

_____

37. The Battle for the Blessing

In this lesson, we will see the outcome of Jacob's deceit in obtaining Esau's blessing and how God's will is completed despite the manipulations of men. (Genesis 27:1-46)

Intro – Review _____

_____

_____

I. The Deception – Genesis 27:1-25

Vs. 1-5 _____

_____

Interesting notes about the blessing.

- Done in _____

_____

_____

- Despite Esau's unholy behavior _____

_____

_____

- Physical blindness = _____

_____

_____

_____

Vs. 6-17 _____

_____

_____

Vs. 18-29 - Why did God allow this? _____

_____

_____

Sometimes it's a question of a lesson of two evils. _____

_____

These situations demonstrate how we need God's _____ in every situation.

_____

_____

In the end the blessing goes to Jacob. _____

_____

Vs. 30-33 _____

_____

What happens to Isaac:

1. Loves Esau _____

_____

2. God shows Isaac that _____

_____

3. Trembling indicates _____

_____

Vs. 34-40 _____

_____

Vs. 41-46 _____

_____

Lessons

1. We need _____

_____

_____

2. Blind love _____

_____

_____

3. There is always _____

_____

_____

38. Jacob's Family

In this section of Genesis, we learn how Jacob came to have two wives who would, in addition to their female slaves, bear the 12 sons of Jacob. (Genesis 28:1-30:24)

Intro – Esau and Jacob are divided because of Jacob's deception.

_____

_____

_____

I. The Blessing

Genesis 28:1-5 _____

_____

_____

_____

II. Esau's Reaction

Genesis 28:6-9 _____

_____

_____

_____

III. Jacob's Ladder

Genesis 28:10-15 _____

_____

_____

_____

_____

Ladder imagery suggests:

1. Movement _____

   _____

2. Angels _____

   _____

3. The Ladder _____

   _____

Genesis 28:16-22 _____

_____

IV. Jacob and Laban

Genesis 29:1-6 _____

_____

Genesis 29:7-12 _____

_____

Genesis 29:13-19 _____

_____

Genesis 29:20-30 _____

_____

V. Jacob's Sons

Genesis 29:31-35_____

_____

_____

_____

Leah

1. _____   _____
2. _____   _____
3. _____   _____
4. _____   _____

Genesis 30:1-8 _____

_____

Bilhah

- _____   _____
- _____   _____

Genesis 30:9-13 _____

_____

Zilpah

- _____   _____
- _____   _____

Genesis 30:14-21 _____

_____

Leah

- _____   _____
- _____   _____
- _____   _____
- _____   _____

Genesis 30:22-24 _____

_____

Rachel

_____   _____

*_____   _____

Lessons

1. God is interested in _____ problems.

_____

_____

_____

_____

2. Giving is part of _____

_____

_____

_____

_____

3. Roll with the _____

_____

_____

_____

_____

39. Jacob Leaves Laban

After 20 years of service, Jacob prepares for his departure from Laban by offering him a potentially lucrative proposal. (Genesis 30:25-31:55)

Intro _____

_____

I. Jacob and Laban's Arrangement – 30:24-43

Jacob has worked for Laban 20 years _____

_____

30:25-28 _____

30:29-34 _____

_____

The Arrangement

1. Laban's Herds _____

_____

2. Jacob's Proposal _____

_____

3. Jacob Proposes _____

_____

    30:35-36 _____

_____

    30:37-43 _____

_____

Jacob's Method

1. Rate of Mating _____

_____

2. Stronger Animals Mated _____

_____

II. Jacob's Departure – Genesis 31

31:1-3 _____

_____

31:17-21 – Jacob departs in haste in fear of Laban. _____

_____

31:22-24 _____

_____

31:25-30 _____

31:31-35 _____

31:36-42 _____

Jacob's Rebuke

Laban's _____

_____

Unfairness _____

_____

Jacob had _____

_____

God's _____

_____

31:43-55 _____

_____

Lessons

1. Put your _____ life in God's hands.

_____

2. Don't let _____ sneak in.

_____

3. Some people don't _____

_____

40. Jacob and Esau - Round 2

After gathering his wives and children and leaving Laban behind, Jacob faces the dangerous confrontation with his brother Esau who had vowed to kill him because of his deception in the matter of the blessing from Isaac. (Genesis 32:1-33:20)

Intro - Review _____

_____

Jacob returns home to face _____.

I. God's Protection Revealed

32:1-2 _____

_____

_____

II. Jacob Prepares to Meet Esau

32:3-8 _____

_____

_____

39:9-12 – Jacob's impossible situation:

- Couldn't _____

- Couldn't _____

- Going forward meant _____

Jacob's Desperate Prayer

32:9 - Calls on the true God.

      Elohim _____

      Jehovah _____

32:10 _____

_____

_____

32:11 _____

_____

_____

32:12 _____

_____

_____

32:13-23 – Jacob begins to demonstrate the intentions of his heart.

_____

_____

III. Jacob Wrestles with God

Wrestling = _____

_____

_____

32:24 _____

_____

_____

32:25 _____

_____

_____

32:26-30 _____

_____

_____

       Jacob = _____

       Israel = _____

32:31-32 _____

_____

_____

_____

IV. Jacob Meets Esau

33:1-7 _____

_____

_____

_____

33:8-11 _____

_____

_____

_____

_____

33:12-17 – Jacob declines Esau's offer for several reasons.

1. _____

2. _____

3. _____

33:18-20 _____

_____

_____

_____

_____

Lessons

1. If God is ___ _____, who _____ _____ _____ you?

_____

_____

_____

2. Pray with all your _____work with all your _____.

_____

_____

_____

3. Where I am _____, I am _____.

_____

_____

_____

41. On the Run Again

After a long period of silence Jacob's story picks up again as his sons cause trouble and we see Jacob in the familiar role of being on the run.
(Genesis 34:1-36:43)

Intro - Review _____

_____

I. The Rape of Dinah – 34:1-31

The problem of raising children in a pagan society.

Vs. 1-4 _____

_____

_____

Vs. 5-18 _____

_____

_____

Vs. 18-24 _____

_____

_____

The Plot

1. Jacob was not _____

_____

_____

2. Ruben and Judah _____

_____

_____

3. The two leaders were _____

_____

_____

4. No respect for circumcision _____

_____

_____

Vs. 25-31 _____

_____

II. Jacob's Renewal – 35:1-29

Vs. 1-4 _____

_____

Renewal of Jacob's family.

1. Purified _____

_____

_____

2. Rededicated _____

_____

_____

3. Redirection _____

_____

_____

Vs. 5-8 _____

_____

_____

_____

Vs. 9-15 – Promise Renewed

1. Jacob was a _____

   _____

   _____

   _____

2. Great nations _____

   _____

   _____

   _____

3. The land _____

   _____

   _____

   _____

Vs. 16-20 _____

_____

_____

_____

Vs. 21-26 _____

_____

_____

_____

Vs. 27-29 _____

_____

_____

_____

III. Esau's Descendants – 36:1-43

_____

_____

_____

_____

Lessons

1. You marry _____

_____

_____

_____

2. Leadership abhors a _____

_____

_____

_____

3. Renewal requires continual _____

_____

_____

_____

42. The Beginning of the End

This lesson begins the story of Joseph, Jacob's son with Rachel, who will become the bridge for the family's travel to and 400-year settlement in Egypt. (Genesis 37:1-36)

Intro – After the rededication of his family, Jacob and his family head back to

their ancestral home.

_____

_____

_____

I. A New Writer – Genesis 37:1-2a

_____

_____

II. Joseph and His Dreams – Genesis 37:2b-11

Vs. 2b-4 – Joseph was Jacob's favorite.

_____

_____

Vs. 5-8 _____

_____

Vs. 9-11 – Jacob has a similar dream. _____

_____

_____

III. Joseph Sold into Slavery – vs. 37:12-36

Vs. 12-14 _____

_____

Vs. 15-17 _____

_____

_____

Vs. 18-22 – Sin has no age or culture. _____

_____

They don't want to shed blood because God will require it of them.

_____

Vs. 23-28 _____

_____

Vs. 29-33 _____

_____

Vs. 34-36 – Jacob's response is total and inconsolable grief. _____

_____

_____

Term "OFFICER" in Hebrew is "SARIS" which means Eunuch.

_____

_____

Lessons

1. Be careful how you use your spiritual gifts. _____

   _____

   _____

   _____

2. We all need refinement. _____

   _____

   _____

   _____

3. Sometimes you have to stand up for right. _____

   _____

   _____

   _____

43. Judah and Tamar

The story of Jacob's family focuses in on one particular son, Judah, through whom the Messiah would eventually come, and examines his unusual relationship with his daughter-in-law Tamar. (Genesis 38:1-30)

Intro - The narrators take a close-up view of Judah through whom

the Messiah would ultimately come. _____

_____

_____

_____

I. Story of Judah – 38:1-30

Vs. 1-5 _____

_____

_____

Vs. 6-10 _____

_____

_____

     Levitate Regulation: _____

     _____

     _____

     _____

     Onanism _____

     _____

     _____

     _____

Bible instruction concerning human sexuality:

- Fidelity – Hebrews 13:4 _____

  _____

  _____

  _____

- Mutual Respect – I Corinthians 7:3-7 _____

  _____

  _____

- Christian Decency – I Thessalonians 4:4 _____

  _____

  _____

Vs. 11-12 _____

_____

_____

_____

Vs. 13-19 _____

_____

_____

_____

Temple Prostitute – Separated one. _____

_____

_____

_____

Judah and Tamar

Judah knew _____

_____

_____

_____

He didn't seek _____ or his _____ for help.

_____

_____

_____

He allowed his _____ to guide him.

_____

_____

_____

_____

Vs. 20-23 _____

_____

_____

Vs. 24-26 _____

_____

_____

Vs. 27-30 _____

_____

_____

_____

Lessons

1. Children are influenced by _____ parents.

_____

_____

_____

_____

_____

2. God can cause _____ things to work for good.

_____

_____

_____

_____

_____

3. It's not who you are, it's who God _____ you.

_____

_____

_____

_____

_____

44. Joseph's Story

After explaining Judah's connection to the coming Messiah, the Genesis writers finish their narrative with the telling of Joseph's story.
(Genesis 39:1-40:23)

Intro - Once Judah's life and his connection to the fulfillment of God's promise to Abraham is explained, the narrative begins to tell Joseph's story.

_____

_____

I. Ancient Egypt

Pharaoh _____

Hyksos _____

Israelites lost favor because: _____

_____

_____

II. Joseph in Potiphar's House

39:1-6 _____

_____

A detailed description of Joseph is given. _____

_____

Vs. 7-10 – Potiphar was an _____.

_____

Joseph is naïve _____

_____

Vs. 11-20 _____

_____

Joseph was not executed _____

_____

_____

Vs. 21-23 _____

_____

III. Joseph in Prison

40:1-4 _____

_____

40:5-8 – Joseph had experienced interpreting dreams. _____

_____

Vs. 9-15 – The butler's dream. _____

_____

Vs. 16-19 – The baker's dream. _____

_____

_____

Vs. 20-23 – Joseph before Pharaoh. _____

_____

_____

Lessons

1. Your boss is _____ _____.

_____

_____

2._____ from temptation.

_____

_____

3. God is a _____ _____.

_____

_____

45. From Prison to Prince

After languishing in prison for several years Joseph is called upon to interpret Pharaoh's dreams and in doing so successfully is transformed from being a prisoner to becoming a prince of Egypt. (Genesis 41:1-57)

Intro - Joseph is falsely accused and is in Potiphar's jail.

_____

_____

I. Pharaoh's Dream – Genesis 41

Vs. 1-7 – Joseph's dreams and those he interpreted seem to come in pairs.

_____

_____

Vs. 8-13 _____

_____

_____

II. Joseph and the Pharaoh

Vs. 14-16 _____

_____

Joseph's 13 years in captivity had taught him patience, restraint and humility.

Vs. 17-24 _____

_____

_____

Vs. 25-32   - 2 dreams represent confirmation

                 - 7 cows / 7 ears represent years of good and bad.

_____

_____

Vs. 33-36 _____

_____

_____

III. Joseph the Chief Official

Vs. 37-45 _____

_____

      All the signs of power are given to Joseph. _____

_____

Vs. 46-52 _____

_____

_____ =

The lesson for us is that God can restore us in a single moment during our lives, or in the "Twinkling of and eye" when Jesus returns. _____

_____

_____

Vs. 53-57 _____

_____

Lessons

1. We're on Gods _____.

_____

_____

2. God _____ the humble and _____ the proud.

_____

_____

3._____ always comes from God.

_____

_____

_____

46. Confrontation

Joseph finally confronts his brothers who initially sold him into slavery.
(Genesis 42:1-44:34)

Intro - Review Joseph's journey from prison to prince.

_____

_____

I. First Trip to Egypt

Twenty years has gone by and Jacob's family is now faced with the famine affecting that region.

42:1-4 _____

_____

_____

Vs. 5-9 – Joseph screens all caravans for two reasons:

1. _____

_____

2._____

_____

Vs. 10-17 – Joseph questions his brothers.

_____

_____

Vs. 18-23 – Joseph keeps one brother as hostage.

_____

_____

Vs. 24-26 _____

_____

_____

Vs. 27-38 – The brothers make an amazing discovery.

_____

_____

II. Second Trip to Egypt

43:1-5 – The famine forces the brothers to make a second trip. _____

_____

Vs. 6-10 – Note some of the changes beginning to take place. _____

_____

Vs. 11-14 – Israel's faith is kindled again. _____

_____

Vs. 15-23 _____

_____

_____

Vs. 24-31 – Joseph reveals himself _____

_____

_____

Vs. 32-34 _____

_____

_____

Lessons

1._____ will find you out.

_____

_____

2. No _____ No _____.

_____

_____

3. Leaders carry the _____ end.

_____

_____

4._____ all you can, leave the rest to _____.

_____

_____

47. Reunion and Reconciliation

After reuniting with his brothers after a separation of 20 years, Joseph lays a plan that will determine if a reconciliation will be possible. (Genesis 45:1-46:27)

Intro - Joseph sets his plan into motion.

_____

_____

I. Joseph Reveals Himself – 45:1

Joseph tests to see if his brothers have changed.

45:1-4 _____

_____

Vs. 5-8 – Joseph wants to do four things:

1. _____
2. _____
3. _____
4. _____

II. Joseph Sends His Brother Home

45:9-15 _____

_____

Vs. 16-20 _____

_____

Vs. 21-24 – Joseph provides gifts. _____

_____

Vs. 25-28 _____

_____

III. Israel in Egypt – 46:1

46:1-4 _____

_____

Advantages in going to Egypt:

1. _____

2. _____

3. _____

4. _____

5. _____

46:5-7 _____

46:8-25 – List of genealogies. _____

_____

46:26-27 _____

_____

The #7 _____

_____

Lessons

1. You _____ _____.

_____

_____

2. God will be _____ when you need _____.

_____

_____

3. Always search for God's will before _____ _____.

_____

_____

God directs us by:

A. _____

B. _____

C. _____

D. _____

48. Family Reunion

This lesson describes the final episode in Joseph's story where Jacob, Joseph and their families are reunited and settled in Egypt. (Genesis 46:27-48:22)

Intro - Review

_____

_____

I. Jacob and Joseph Meet – 46:28-34

Vs. 46:28-30 _____

_____

Vs. 31-34 _____

_____

Joseph stresses their occupation as shepherds:

1. _____

_____

2. _____

_____

II. Jacob and the Pharaoh – 47:1-12

Vs. 47:1-6 _____

Vs. 7-10 _____

Vs. 11-12 _____

_____

III. The Famine Continues – 47:13-26

Vs. 13-21 – The effects of the famine _____

_____

_____

Vs. 22-26 – Arrangements between the Pharaoh and the people. _____

_____

IV. Last Days of Jacob – 47:27-31

_____

_____

V. Jacob Blesses Joseph's Sons – 48:1-22

Vs. 1-4 _____

_____

Vs. 5-7 – Firstborn privileges transferred from Ruben to Joseph.

1. _____

2. _____

3. _____

Vs. 8-12 _____

_____

Vs. 13-16 _____

_____

Vs. 17-20 _____

_____

Vs. 21-22 _____

_____

Lessons

1. God's ways _____

_____

_____

2. God can prosper you _____

_____

_____

3. God chooses for _____

_____

_____

49. Jacob's Prophecies

At the end of his life Jacob gives each of his sons a prophecy concerning their future. This event along with the death of both Jacob and Joseph will close out the Genesis record. (Genesis 49:11-50:26)

Intro – The writers describe two significant meetings that take place.

1. _____

2. _____

I. Prophecy Concerning the Tribes – 49:1-27

Jacob gives each son a prophecy concerning their future:

1. Ruben – vs. 3-4 _____

2. Simeon and Levi – vs. 5-7 _____

3. Judah – vs. 8-12

   - Judah's name means _____

   - The "scepter" would not pass from Judah until "Shiloh" came. _____
   _____

4. Zebulun and Issachar – vs. 13-15 _____
_____
_____

5. Dan – vs. 16-18 _____
_____
_____

6. Gad, Ashur, Naphtali – vs. 19-21 _____
_____
_____

7. Joseph – vs. 22-26 _____
_____
_____

8. Benjamin – vs. 27 _____
_____
_____

II. Jacob's Last Words – 49:28-33

_____

_____

III. Jacob's Burial – Genesis 50:1-21

Vs. 1-3 _____

Vs. 4-9 _____

Vs. 10-14 _____

Vs. 15-21 _____

_____

Joseph reassures his brothers in two ways:

      A. _____

      B. _____

IV. Joseph's Death – 50:22-26

Vs. 22-23 _____

Vs. 24-26 _____

_____

Lessons

1. Nothing stops _____

_____

_____

2. _____ are deceiving.

_____

_____

3. God forgives and forgets _____

_____

_____

50. Final Summary

In this last lesson Mike will wrap up this long study by sharing three key lessons taught to us by Genesis.

Intro - Stats

- 1 year _____

- 1,533 verses _____

- 4th _____

- Genesis Record _____

- 700 _____

- 600 _____

_____

_____

I. Key Lessons

Lesson #1 _____

_____

_____

Genesis helps us make sense of the world.

A. _____

B. _____

C. _____

D. _____

E. _____

Some Christians have begun to change their view of Genesis in order

to accommodate new theories. _____

_____

_____

Lesson #2 _____

_____

_____

_____

A. Generous _____

_____

_____

B. Thoughtful _____

_____

_____

C. Merciful _____

_____

_____

Lesson #3 _____

_____

_____

_____

Genesis 15:5-6 _____

_____

_____

In the New Testament, God still requires obedience to demonstrate faith.

_____

_____

_____

Summary

This has been a long and in-depth course of study. _____
_____
_____

We've learned that Genesis is a book that:

- Covers _____
- Reveals _____
- Shows _____

_____
_____
_____
_____
_____
_____
_____
_____
_____
_____

> **“**

BibleTalk.tv is one of the **most-prolific uploaders** on Amazon Prime Video with more videos than any major Hollywood studio except Paramount Pictures.

THE WALL STREET JOURNAL.

BibleTalk.tv is an Internet Mission Work.

We provide textual Bible teaching material on our website and mobile apps for free. We enable churches and individuals all over the world to have access to high quality Bible materials for personal growth, group study or for teaching in their classes.

The goal of this mission work is to spread the gospel to the greatest number of people using the latest technology available. For the first time in history it is becoming possible to preach the gospel to the entire world at once. BibleTalk.tv is an effort to preach the gospel to all nations every day until Jesus returns.

The Choctaw Church of Christ in Oklahoma City is the sponsoring congregation for this work and provides the oversight for the BibleTalk ministry team. If you would like information on how you can support this ministry, please go to the link provided below.

bibletalk.tv/support